JOHN H. TAYLOR

EGYPTIAN COFFINS

D1642506

SHIRE EGYPTOLOGY

2

British Library Cataloguing in Publication Data.
Taylor, John H.
Egyptian Coffins. — (Shire Egyptology)
1. Ancient Egyptian. Coffins
I. Title
736'.4
ISBN 0-85263-977-5

Published by
SHIRE PUBLICATIONS LTD
Cromwell House, Church Street, Princes Risborough,
Aylesbury, Bucks HP17 9AJ, UK.

Series Editor: Barbara Adams

ISBN 0 85263 977 5

First published 1989.

Set in 11 point Times and printed in Great Britain by
C.I. Thomas & Sons (Haverfordwest) Ltd,
Press Buildings, Merlins Bridge,
Haverfordwest, Dyfed.

Contents

4

List of illustrations

Chronology

Predynastic and Protodynastic	before 3050 BC		
Early Dynastic or Archaic Period	3050 to 2686 BC	3050-2890	Dynasty I
		2890-2686	Dynasty II
Old Kingdom	2686 to 2181 BC	2686-2613	Dynasty III
		2668-2649	*Djoser*
		2613-2498	Dynasty IV
		2498-2345	Dynasty V
		2345-2181	Dynasty VI
First Intermediate Period	2181 to 2040 BC	2181-2040	Dynasties VII-X
		2134-2060	Dynasty XI (1)
Middle Kingdom	2040 to 1782 BC	2060-1991	Dynasty XI (2)
		2060-2010	*Mentuhotep II*
		1991-1782	Dynasty XII
Second Intermediate Period	1782 to 1570 BC	1782-1650	Dynasties XIII-XIV (Egyptian)
		1663-1555	Dynasties XV-XVI (Hyksos)
		1663-1570	Dynasty XVII (Theban)
			Nubkheperre Intef
New Kingdom	1570 to 1070 BC	1570-1293	Dynasty XVIII
		1570-1546	*Ahmose*
		1551-1524	*Amenophis I*
		1524-1518	*Tuthmosis I*
		1504-1450	*Tuthmosis III*
		1498-1483	*Hatshepsut*
		1386-1349	*Amenophis III*
		1334-1325	*Tutankhamun*
		1293-1185	Dynasty XIX
		1291-1278	*Seti I*
		1279-1212	*Ramesses II*
		1185-1070	Dynasty XX
		1098-1070	*Ramesses XI*

6

Third Intermediate Period	1070 to 713 BC		
		1070-945	Dynasty XXI
		1039-991	*Psusennes I*
		945-712	Dynasty XXII
		924-889	*Osorkon I*
		890	*Shoshenq II*
		874-850	*Osorkon II*
		870-860	*Harsiese*
		828-712	Dynasty XXIII
		724-713	Dynasty XXIV
Late Period	713 to 332 BC		
		713-656	Dynasty XXV
		664-525	Dynasty XXVI
		525-404	Dynasty XXVII
		404-399	Dynasty XXVIII
		399-380	Dynasty XXIX
		380-343	Dynasty XXX
		343-332	Dynasty XXXI
Graeco-Roman Period	332 BC to AD 395		
		332-30	Ptolemaic Dynasty
		30 BC-AD 395	Roman Emperors

1
Purpose and symbolic significance

Coffins are among the most fascinating and attractive of ancient Egyptian antiquities, but their very popularity, together with the sensational associations which they have acquired, has tended to make Egyptologists shy away from studying them. This is regrettable, for not only can they tell us much of value concerning the materials and techniques used by the ancient craftsmen, but they constitute one of the richest sources of information about the Egyptians' religious concepts, providing a wealth of pictorial and textual evidence for the development of beliefs about the afterlife.

This book aims to present an outline of the stylistic evolution of coffins, while attempting at the same time to give some explanation of the changes in their form and decoration. The attribution of coffins to the main phases of Egyptian civilisation is relatively easy, since the shape and general appearance usually provide a rough guide. But to determine the date of a coffin more precisely evidence of all kinds has to be taken into account: the archaeological context, the constructional techniques, the layout of the designs, the colour scheme employed, the decorative subject matter, the iconography of gods, goddesses and religious symbols, the choice of texts used, and so on, while to make matters more complicated some stylistic features were deliberately revived long after their original appearance.

To understand the changes in coffin style over the centuries it is important to have some knowledge of the religious factors which influenced their development. The coffin was primarily a container for the corpse, to protect it from destruction by scavenging animals or tomb robbers, but already in very early times it had a religious role to fulfil, the aim of which was the protection of the deceased and the ensuring of his well-being in the afterlife.

The coffin was given the means to do this in two ways: by the symbolic power inherent in its shape and by painting and inscribing on it specific religious scenes and texts, the magical presence of which around the mummy would achieve the desired effects. Because of the peculiar nature of Egyptian religious attitudes, whereby two or more mutually contradictory views of the afterlife could be held side by side, the texts and scenes on a particular coffin are often drawn from more than one different mythological source. Full analysis of the iconography and symbolism of coffins can be very complex and here we can only touch on the main factors which influenced their form and decoration.

The coffin as an eternal dwelling

According to one of the earliest concepts of the afterlife, the grave or tomb acted as the deceased's eternal dwelling place. The superstructures of the great brick tombs of the Early Dynastic Period reflected this in their external decoration — a kind of recessed panelling which was based on the forms of primitive domestic architecture. The earliest symbolic role of the coffin was simply an extension of this idea; it, too, acted as a 'house' for the owner's spirit and was adorned with a vaulted top and panelling analogous to that of the tombs (chapter 2). The tomb also satisfied the dead person's need for nourishment and other essentials by incorporating into its structure an offering chapel, the focal point of which was the 'false door' stela. Food and drink were regularly laid before this by the deceased's relatives or mortuary priests, and the false door served as a magical portal through which the spirit of the dead man could pass from the burial chamber on the western side of the tomb into the chapel on the east to partake of the offerings. In case the provision of offerings should be discontinued, lists of the desired commodities and scenes showing servants producing food and drink were carved on the chapel walls. These texts and pictures could, at the master's command, magically act as substitutes for the things represented.

Towards the end of the Old Kingdom the most important of these magical aids began to be depicted on the insides of the coffin, as if they duplicated the walls of the tomb itself. At first this was perhaps just intended as a way of making doubly sure that the owner did not go hungry. Between the Old and Middle Kingdoms, however, the disturbed state of the country led to a serious decline in the practice of decorating tombs and it became increasingly common for the most essential material to be painted on the coffin. In this way the coffin came to be in some respects a miniature version of the tomb, and while its role as a 'house' faded into obscurity the painting of its inner surfaces with major funerary texts and pictures continued, even after the revival of tomb decoration in the Middle Kingdom.

The solar and Osirian concepts of the afterlife

From the Old Kingdom onwards funerary beliefs and practices were primarily based on two alternative doctrines and allusions to these account for a large part of coffin decoration in the subsequent periods. According to the earlier view the dead ascended to heaven and joined Re, the sun god, accompanying him in his perpetual journeys across the sky by day and through the subterranean

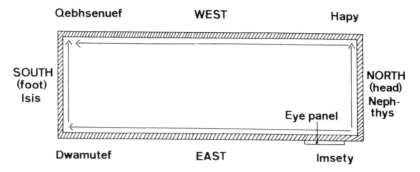

1. Plan of a rectangular coffin showing positions of major deities. The arrows indicate the direction in which the inscriptions are to be read.

netherworld by night. Depictions of the god (usually in the hybrid form of the falcon-headed Re-Harakhty), the winged sun disk and the solar barque are commonly encountered on coffins, particularly after the New Kingdom. Representations of the sunrise (a symbol of rebirth) are also frequent, the favourite image showing the scarab beetle, Khepri, pushing the solar disk.

By the Middle Kingdom the myth of Osiris had become the predominant influence on beliefs about the afterlife. Osiris, murdered by his brother Seth, was restored to life again through the agency of Isis, Nephthys, Horus and Thoth, and every individual hoped, by being identified with Osiris, to enjoy resurrection after death, as the god had done. According to mythology, Osiris was protected by his wife, Isis, and her sister, Nephthys, who were stationed at the foot and head of his bier. Thus, after the Old Kingdom, inscriptions naming these goddesses (and later, figures of them) began to appear at the foot and head of the coffin to emphasise the occupant's identification with Osiris.

Further protection was provided by the four sons of Horus — Imsety, Hapy, Dwamutef and Qebhsenuef; their speeches and later their figures were painted on the long sides of the coffin and they are often accompanied by invocations to other major deities of the Osirian cycle, such as Geb, Nut, Shu and Tefnut, so that the deceased was completely surrounded by a ring of divine protection. The coffin was usually orientated in the tomb with the sides facing the four cardinal points and the positioning of the principal deities on the walls followed a fixed pattern, already well established by the Middle Kingdom (figure 1). Chapter 151 of the Book of the Dead has a vignette which shows these divinities grouped around the mummy in the same relative positions which they

2. Osiris in the temple of Seti I, Abydos.

occupy on the coffins. Here we see not only Isis and Nephthys and the sons of Horus, but also two forms of Anubis, whose speeches and figures appear in the middle of the coffin sides in the New Kingdom.

The goddess Nut

Nut, the sky goddess, was of great importance as a protector of the dead at least as early as the Old Kingdom. Her funerary associations are twofold. On the one hand she was regarded as the mother of the deceased through his identification with Osiris (the son of Nut). The goddess could be symbolically identified with the coffin and so, when the dead man was sealed inside this, it was as if he was being placed within the body of Nut, his divine mother, thereby reaching a state from which he could begin a new life. Indeed, in texts of the Old Kingdom the word for the chest of a sarcophagus is *mwt* ('mother') — a clear allusion to this concept — while on the interiors of many coffins of the Libyan Period a figure of the goddess appears, extending her arms as if to embrace the mummy.

Nut's other important role, as sky goddess, led to her close association with the coffin lid. This lay above the mummy, just as Nut was supposed to stretch her star-studded body over the earth. In an important prayer, first found in the Pyramid Texts, the goddess is beseeched to spread herself over the deceased in a gesture of protection: 'O my mother Nut, spread yourself over me, so that I may be placed among the imperishable stars and may never die.' Versions of this text were commonly written on coffin and sarcophagus lids and, beginning in the New Kingdom, figures of Nut in various protective attitudes were also depicted.

Anthropoid coffins

Each of the two main types of coffin — rectangular and anthropoid — originally had a different magical function. When anthropoid coffins first appeared, in the Twelfth Dynasty, they simply copied the appearance of the mummy and served as a substitute body in which the owner's spirit could reside if the real body were destroyed (the same idea supplied the motivation for the provision of tomb statues and the earliest shabtis).

On a different level, the anthropoid coffin was an image of the deceased as a *sah,* or divine being, with shining golden skin (hence the gilded faces of the finest specimens). At first this divine quality was not associated with any particular god. However, the popularity of the anthropoid coffin increased greatly from the New Kingdom, largely, one suspects, because it came to be regarded as a representation of the deceased in the guise of Osiris. The traditional image of the god was based on the appearance of a mummified body (figure 2), just as was the coffin, and so the use of such a case helped to emphasise the link between its occupant and the deity. With the passage of time the anthropoid coffin acquired other features taken from the iconography of Osiris: the curled 'divine' beard, the hands crossed on the breast and, occasionally, the green face. In the New Kingdom the anthropoid cases also took over the symbolic functions of the rectangular coffins; these became virtually obsolete in the Eighteenth Dynasty and the motifs and designs belonging to them were interwoven with elements deriving from the anthropoid coffin's other roles.

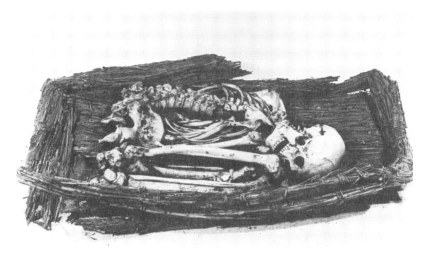

3. Contracted burial in a reed basket. Tarkhan, *c.*3000 BC. (Courtesy of the Trustees of the British Museum; 52887.)

4. 'House' coffin for a contracted burial. Tarkhan, Second or Third Dynasty. (Cairo JE 43794; after Petrie, Wainwright and Gardiner, *Tarkhan I and Memphis V*, London, 1913, plate XXVIII.)

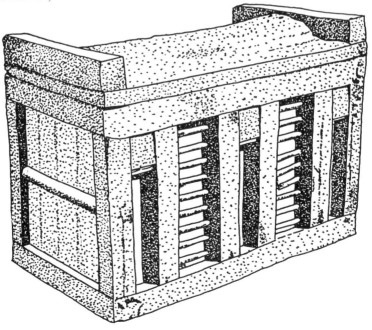

2
The Early Dynastic Period and the Old Kingdom

In the early Predynastic Period (from $c.4500$ BC) the majority of the dead were buried lying on their sides in a contracted posture, in simple oval pits, the heads pointing southwards and the faces turned towards the west (towards the setting sun and what was traditionally regarded as the land of the dead). Mummification was as yet unknown, but even at this period efforts were made to protect the bodies from decomposition by providing them with some kind of covering; at first they were wrapped in reed matting or animal skins, but later in the Predynastic Period use was made of baskets or large pots, which were usually inverted over the corpse (figure 3). Simple clay coffins, oval or rectangular in shape, were also used in some cemeteries. Towards the end of the fourth millennium BC the desire to improve conditions for the dead led to the introduction of rectangular brick-lined sepulchres with levelled floors and a roofing of logs, while the bodies were often wrapped in linen bandages. In some graves (as at Matmar and El Mahasna) a wooden framework, sometimes covered with mats, was erected around the body. It is not always clear whether these frameworks were intended as linings for the sides of the grave or as containers for the corpse, but they are of interest since it was probably from them that the first wooden coffins evolved.

With the introduction of copper tools in the late Predynastic Period the Egyptians made their first attempts at woodworking, leading to the appearance of the earliest true coffins. These were rectangular chests, made of rough pieces of wood dowelled together, which, because of the custom of burying the dead in the contracted position, were relatively short: 1 metre long on average. Many were nothing more than plain boxes, but others carried a distinctive type of decoration (figure 4). The lid was curved or vaulted, with a rectangular board at each end, and one or more of the sides was decorated with a series of niches imitating the recessed panelling ('palace facade') of early dwellings. This emphasised the symbolic function of these coffins as 'houses' for the spirit (chapter 1).

These panelled coffins seem to have been introduced in the Second or Third Dynasty and examples are known from the cemeteries at Saqqara, Tarkhan and Beni Hasan. Parts of the Tarkhan coffins had clearly been used before: some pieces were found to contain old joint-holes, while others had been weathered on one face, suggesting that they had once formed part of structures which had stood exposed to the elements for a long time.

The Old Kingdom

By the beginning of the Fourth Dynasty significant advances in embalming techniques were being made, notably with the introduction of the practice of eviscerating the corpse. The embalming could be done more efficiently with the body stretched out on its back and from about the Third or Fourth Dynasty it became more and more common for corpses to be buried in this position. Consequently, the short box-coffins were replaced by longer cases, designed to contain bodies buried in the extended position.

Members of the royal family were probably among the first to adopt this new style of burial. In chambers beneath the Step Pyramid of King Djoser at Saqqara (Third Dynasty) were found two alabaster sarcophagi, one of which contained the skeleton of a child in a plywood coffin of the 'long' type. The coffin was constructed from small pieces of various different types of wood, arranged in six very thin layers with the grain running alternately lengthways and crossways to give added strength. The outer surface had been carved with vertical striations and gilded. The gilding had been torn off by robbers but some fragments remained, still held in place by the original gold nails.

The majority of surviving coffins of the Old Kingdom come from Giza and Saqqara. During this period some of the highest-ranking courtiers and officials were provided with a stone sarcophagus and a wooden coffin, while others were buried in two wooden coffins, one inside the other — a practice which continued and developed over the centuries. The exact reason for the doubling of the coffin is unknown; perhaps the outer case was a cheaper substitute for a sarcophagus or it may have been intended simply to give extra protection to the mummy. Humbler persons had to be content with only one coffin and these generally consisted of a patchwork of irregularly shaped pieces, dowelled together. Throughout the pharaonic period native woods were most often used for making coffins, the most popular being the sycamore fig (*Ficus sycomorus*), the tamarisk and the acacia. For those who could afford them, imported timbers such as Lebanese cedar were available. Although expensive, this wood was relatively easy to work and straight planks of large size could be obtained; the lid of the coffin of Setka from Giza (Cairo J. 49696) was made from a single piece. Moreover, cedar was less prone to destruction by termites (which avoid resinous coniferous wood) than were native timbers such as acacia — an advantage which was perhaps unforeseen by the Egyptians. Other imported woods used for coffins included cypress, fir, juniper, lime, pine and yew.

The simplest Old Kingdom coffins were smooth-sided and perfectly plain. However, two decorated types were also in use at this period. One had recessed panelling and a vaulted lid and was derived directly from the Early Dynastic 'house' coffins. This type remained in use as late as the Sixth Dynasty. A fine example with panelled decoration, dating to the early Fifth Dynasty, was found in the mastaba of Seshathotep at Giza (Cairo J. 49695).

With the introduction of the second decorated type in the early Sixth Dynasty the basic design elements which were to be used in coffin decoration for the next eight centuries were established (figure 5). The Sixth Dynasty examples, such as that of Idu II from Giza, have a smooth-sided case and a flat lid, down the centre of which is an inscription. Around the upper edge of the case, both inside and out, is a horizontal band containing the 'offering formula' — an invocation to provide the deceased with sustenance and other necessities in the afterlife. The rest of the decoration was also functional. For religious reasons, great importance was attached to the orientation of the corpse. In the Old and Middle Kingdoms the coffin was normally positioned in the burial chamber with the head pointing northwards and the long left side towards the east, so that the mummy, placed on its left side within the coffin, faced towards the part of the tomb where the funerary offerings were made and towards the land of the living. As a mag-

5. Coffin of Nebhotep, constructed from irregularly shaped planks and decorated with eyes for the dead man to look through. Sixth Dynasty. (Courtesy of the Trustees of the British Museum; 46629.)

ical aid for the deceased, a pair of eyes was painted or carved on the
exterior head end of the coffin's eastern side. It was believed that
the dead man could look out through these eyes into the tomb, thus
maintaining a link with the world of the living, and special care was
taken to ensure that the mummy's face was correctly aligned with
the 'eye panel'. Because of its symbolic associations, the eastern
wall was the most important part of the coffin and it was here that
most of the other decoration appeared, adapted from the kind of
ornamentation found on the walls of burial chambers and offering
chapels of the late Old Kingdom. On the interior of the coffin,
behind the eye panel, was a depiction of a false door, to enable the
spirit of the occupant to pass freely in and out to receive his offerings. A list of these offerings was painted next to the false door, and
on some specimens (such as that of Idu II) the northern end wall
bore a depiction of the Seven Sacred Oils used in the ritual of the
Opening of the Mouth.

The position of the mummy's head was of paramount importance and determined the arrangement of the external inscriptions.
The offering formulae around the coffin commence at the north-
east corner, nearest to the face, and proceed towards the foot end
(figure 1). The inscription on the lid also runs from head to foot and
when, in the Middle Kingdom, figures of deities began to be
painted on the sides, they were carefully positioned so as to face
towards the all-important eye panel. The importance attached to
orientating the coffin properly in the tomb is seen in the fact that on
some of these Old Kingdom specimens hieroglyphic signs for
'head', 'foot' or 'south' have been found, inscribed on the appropriate side to assist the undertakers in their task.

3
The First Intermediate Period and the Middle Kingdom

The coffins of the First Intermediate Period and the Middle Kingdom evolved from the painted and inscribed type of the Sixth Dynasty and, although they display greater stylistic variety, they share a number of common features. The rectangular shape remained standard and the inscriptions down the centre of the lid and around the edge of the case continued to be the main external decoration. The text on the lid is usually an offering formula addressed to Anubis, while the horizontal inscriptions on the sides are invocations to Osiris, Anubis, Isis and Nephthys. The sides were now also subdivided into panels by vertical inscriptions spaced at regular intervals — usually four on each long side and one or two on the short sides. These texts ensured the protection of other deities, notably Geb, Nut, Shu, Tefnut and the sons of Horus.

The eye panel was still the most important feature of the external decoration, but it had now acquired a secondary function: to enable the deceased to see the sun rising on the eastern horizon. This is made clear by an inscription above the eye panel on the coffin of Sebekaa (Twelfth Dynasty): 'Opened is the face of this Sebekaa, so that he may see the Lord of the Horizon when he crosses over the sky . . .'

The constructional methods used on these coffins were much the same as those of the Old Kingdom. The poorer-quality specimens were made of irregular pieces of native wood, whereas those of high officials were carefully assembled from large, regularly shaped planks of imported timber. The components were secured at the corners by mitre joints and wooden dowels, and cords were sometimes threaded through the dowel-holes to help hold the planks together. The floor fitted inside the four walls and the completed coffin rested on four transverse battens which gave added strength and solidity.

The precise dating of coffins within this period is still impossible, but regional styles can be recognised. Throughout the Old Kingdom Memphis had been the chief centre of artistic production, but after the collapse of the Memphite monarchy, c.2181 BC, provincial schools of sculpture and painting arose in all parts of Egypt, each having its own local peculiarities. In the decoration of coffins two main traditions can be distinguished: a northern or Lower

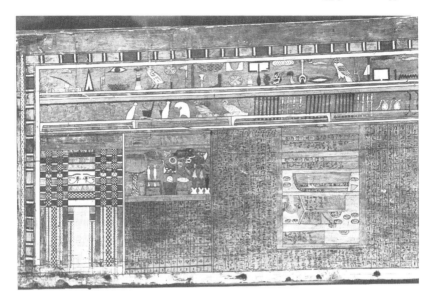

6. Eastern wall (interior) of the inner coffin of Gua showing object frieze, false door, funeral meal and extracts from the Coffin Texts. El Bersha, Eleventh or Twelfth Dynasty. (Courtesy of the Trustees of the British Museum; 30840.)

Egyptian type, which is found in the Memphite area and in Middle Egypt, north of Thebes; and a southern or Upper Egyptian type, which occurs at Asyut and sites to the south of this.

The northern type of coffin

Some of the best examples of this type come from the Memphite necropolis, from Beni Hasan, El Bersha and Meir. On the earlier examples the external decoration consists only of the eye panel and text bands. The interiors of these coffins, however, were much more elaborately decorated than those of their Old Kingdom precursors, all four walls being painted in bright colours. The false door continued to appear on the east side at the head end (figure 6). Next to this there is often a representation of the funeral meal, and the offering list appears on the same side. On the western wall is typically found the 'frieze of objects', a narrow band filled with pictures of commodities of all kinds: clothing, jewellery, sceptres, staves, tools, weapons, religious emblems, games, furniture and vessels, all meticulously detailed and labelled with their names (figure 7). The pictures represented the objects which it was

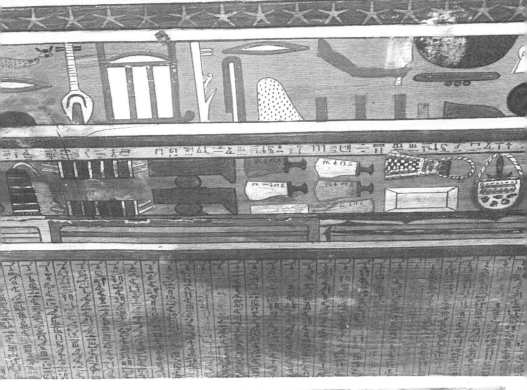

7. Western wall (interior) of the inner coffin of Seni showing object frieze and Coffin Texts. El Bersha, Eleventh or Twelfth Dynasty. (Courtesy of the Trustees of the British Museum; 30842.)

8. End wall (interior) of the outer coffin of Gua showing vessels, clothing and granaries. El Bersha, Eleventh or Twelfth Dynasty. (Courtesy of the Trustees of the British Museum; 30839.)

Egyptian Coffins

thought the deceased might have need of and which, like the scenes sculpted on the tomb walls, could act as magical substitutes for the things depicted. The pictures often continue on the short ends of the coffin. At the head are the sacred oils, a row of granaries to ensure a perpetual supply of food (figure 8) and, appropriately, one or more headrests. Sandals were usually shown at the foot.

Besides the object frieze, the most distinctive characteristic of the coffins of this period was the occurrence, again on the interior, of the Coffin Texts, written in cursive hieroglyphs in narrow columns. These were magical spells, derived mainly from the royal

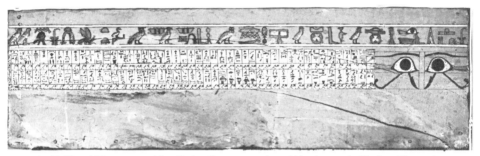

9. Coffin of Nemty-wy with offering list on exterior. Akhmim, probably late Eleventh Dynasty. (Courtesy of the Visitors of the Ashmolean Museum, Oxford; 1911.477.)

10. Inner coffin of Nakhti from Tomb 7 at Asyut, probably Eleventh Dynasty. (Louvre E. 11936; from Chassinat and Palanque, *Une Campagne de Fouilles dans la Nécropole d'Assi-out*, Cairo, 1911, plate XVI.)

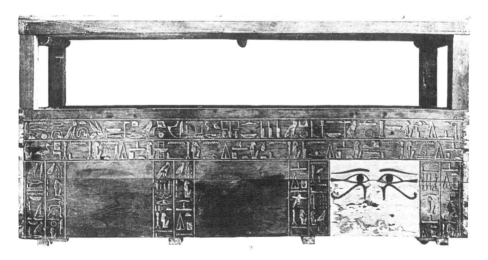

Pyramid Texts of the Old Kingdom, and were designed to ensure the well-being of the deceased in the netherworld. They include the earliest surviving versions of many spells which were later incorporated into the Book of the Dead, but historically the most remarkable aspect of the Coffin Texts is the 'democratisation' of the afterlife which they reveal. In them we see religious material which originally was the prerogative only of the king being made available to the ordinary people, who could therefore now enjoy the same privileges after death as the Pharaoh.

The southern type of coffin
   The decoration of the southern or Upper Egyptian coffins is confined mainly to the exterior. Unlike the northern type, they frequently bear scenes in which human figures appear. Examples have been found at Asyut, Akhmim, Thebes, Gebelein and El Moalla, and the regional peculiarities of each type are well defined. Coffins made at Akhmim are recognisable by the prominent painting of the offering list on the eastern side, next to the eye panel (figure 9). In the Theban area domestic scenes are frequent. The stone sarcophagi of Mentuhotep II's wives, from Deir el-Bahri, have fine depictions of granaries, cows suckling calves and being milked, and the owner having her hair dressed while being waited on by attendants. Similar hairdressing scenes are found on wooden coffins from Gebelein and El Moalla, a little to the south of Thebes, and these also carry representations of beer brewing, butchery and the mummy on a bier.
   On coffins from Asyut the offering formulae around the edge of the case often occupy two lines instead of one, and the vertical text columns may also be grouped in pairs (figure 10). As usual, the first compartment on the eastern side contains the two eyes. The other panels may be blank, but on some examples those on the western side contain extracts from the offering list (figure 11) and figured scenes may also occur. On the short ends the sons of Horus are sometimes represented as squatting figures — the earliest depictions of deities on coffins. Several coffins from Asyut, Thebes, Gebelein and Aswan have astronomical texts painted on the underside of the lid. These texts consist of the names of various stars and constellations arranged in a grid of small compartments and were intended to provide a rough method of measuring time during the night (figure 12). In addition, four important figures are depicted in a row and are invoked in an accompanying text for the deceased's benefit. One is Nut, supporting the vault of heaven above her head; another the goddess Sopdet (Sothis), who repre-

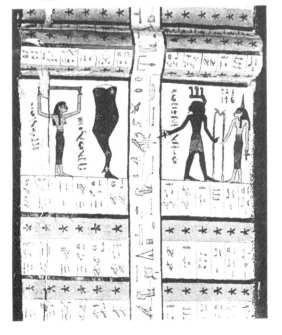

11. Coffin of Hepdjefa with object frieze and offering list on exterior. Asyut, First Intermediate Period. (From Chassinat and Palanque, *Une Campagne de Fouilles dans la Nécropole d'Assiout*, Cairo, 1911, plate XL.)

12. Astronomical 'clock' on the lid of the coffin of Khety. Asyut, First Intermediate Period. (Louvre E. 12036; from Chassinat and Palanque, *Une Campagne de Fouilles dans la Nécropole d'Assiout*, Cairo, 1911, plate XXV.)

sents the star Sirius. The other two figures personify the constellations of Orion (shown as a man turning his head) and Ursa Major (known to the Egyptians as the 'Bull's Foreleg').

The later Middle Kingdom

The exact course of stylistic development followed by the Middle Kingdom rectangular coffins is still unclear, but it appears that the external decoration became more complex as time passed. In the later Twelfth Dynasty a false door was commonly represented below the eye panel (figure 13) and this led to the custom of filling the remaining spaces between the vertical inscriptions with elaborately painted false-door motifs. Excellent examples of this style are the coffins of the 'Two Brothers' from Rifeh (Manchester Museum) and those of Mentuhotep from Thebes (Berlin 9-11). Other innovations of this period included the painting of cavetto cornice designs around the top of the coffin (figure 14) and the appearance of the figures of Isis and Nephthys on the short sides (figure 15). On some examples, such as the outer coffin of Mentuhotep, the lid sloped from head to foot like the roof of a shrine.

The earliest anthropoid coffins

Probably towards the end of the Twelfth Dynasty the first anthropoid coffins appeared: mummiform cases comprising a front and back which fitted securely together, enveloping the body completely. It is believed that this new type of coffin developed from the cartonnage masks which were frequently placed over the heads of mummies in the First Intermediate Period and early Middle

13. Inner coffin of the army commander Sepi. El Bersha, Eleventh or Twelfth Dynasty. (Courtesy of the Trustees of the British Museum; 55315.)

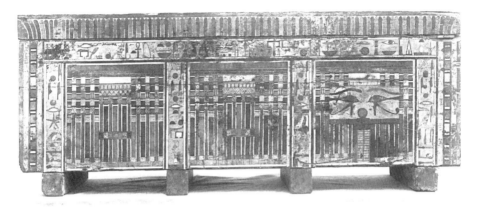

14. Outer coffin of Khnumhotpe from Meir, late Twelfth Dynasty. (Courtesy of the Metropolitan Museum of Art, New York, Rogers Fund, 1912; 12.182.131 B.)

Kingdom. Attempts to convert the mask into a covering which fitted snugly around the whole body were being made as early as the reign of Mentuhotep II, one of whose wives, Queen Ashait, was provided with a cartonnage mummy case. In a tomb at Beni Hasan John Garstang discovered a burial, probably of the Twelfth Dynasty, on which the mask had been extended into a full-length covering. These are isolated instances, however, and the different stages in the evolution of genuine anthropoid coffins are not yet clearly understood.

The first true anthropoid coffins occur in association with the polychrome rectangular cases and the 'court-type' burials of the later Twelfth and Thirteenth Dynasties (chapter 4). They are made of wood or of cartonnage applied to a wooden frame and were carefully modelled to reproduce the contours of the mummified body. The decoration consisted only of features which might be found on the body at this period — the mask, the bead collar and the barrel-shaped *seweret* bead worn on the throat. The faces are often gilded and the eyes inlaid, but the hands are not represented. On some coffins, notably those of the 'Two Brothers', the body is decorated with a brightly coloured reticulated pattern imitating bead netting, but others are simply painted black or white. On some coffins a single line of inscription runs down the front (figure 16). Plain transverse bands, spaced at regular intervals, appear on the lid and continue on the case. These probably represent the outer bindings which held the mummy wrappings in place.

The principal magical function of these early anthropoid coffins seems to have been as a substitute body (chapter 1). As 'copies' of the mummy, they were placed inside rectangular coffins, lying on their left sides so that the face should be aligned with the eye panel on the eastern wall.

15. Figure of Isis on the end wall of the coffin of Khnumnakht from Meir, late Twelfth Dynasty. (Courtesy of the Metropolitan Museum of Art, New York, Rogers Fund, 1915; 15.2.2.)

16. Anthropoid coffin of the warrior Userhet. Beni Hasan, second half of Twelfth Dynasty. (Courtesy of the Fitzwilliam Museum, Cambridge; E.88.1903.)

17. Coffin of Senebni. Qurna, Seventeenth Dynasty. (Cairo CG 28029; from Lacau, *Sarcophages Anterieurs au Nouvel Empire,* Cairo, 1904, plate XV.)

18. *Rishi* coffin of Reri. Dra Abu el-Naga, Seventeenth Dynasty. (Courtesy of the Metropolitan Museum of Art, New York, Rogers Fund, 1912; 12.181.299.)

19. Gilded *rishi* coffin of King Nubkheperre Intef. Dra Abu el-Naga, Seventeenth Dynasty. (Courtesy of the Trustees of the British Museum; 6652.)

4
The Second Intermediate Period and the Eighteenth Dynasty

Stylistically, the coffins of non-royal persons of the early Second Intermediate Period have little to distinguish them from those of the later Twelfth Dynasty. For members of the royal family and high officials, however, a distinctive style of burial (dubbed the 'court type' by Egyptologists) came into fashion in this period. Most of the examples have been found in tombs close to the pyramids of the Twelfth Dynasty kings at Lahun, Lisht and Dahshur, and for many years it was believed that the burials in question were approximately contemporary with those pyramids. More recent research, however, suggests that some should be assigned to the end of the Twelfth Dynasty, while others are undoubtedly of the Thirteenth.

Typical of the 'court type' burials are rectangular coffins of very fine quality but somewhat austere appearance. They have no object friezes or pictorial representations of the kind associated with the later Twelfth Dynasty coffins and the exteriors are severely plain. The intention seems to have been to show off the fine texture of the cedar wood of which most of these coffins were made, and on some examples the decoration consisted only of the eye panel and strips of gold foil along the edges. Others had gilded text bands in the traditional positions, but no false doors were represented. Several of the 'court' coffins had a vaulted lid, similar to those of the 'house' coffins of the Early Dynastic Period and the Old Kingdom. The inner coffin was of the anthropoid type. The masks and collars of these were richly inlaid and sometimes — as in the burial of Senebtisi at Lisht — the whole coffin was sheathed in gold leaf over a coating of linen and plaster. Particular care was taken to prevent the inner coffin being opened once the mummy had been placed inside. A series of metal hooks projected from the edges of the lid; as the lid was slid into place these were engaged in sockets set into the body of the coffin and a metal swivel at the foot end dropped into a slot, effectively sealing the coffin. Since these precautions would hardly thwart determined tomb robbers, one cannot help suspecting that they were there to remove temptation from the undertakers responsible for the burial.

From c. 1650 BC the whole Delta and the northern part of Upper Egypt came under the control of the Hyksos, while the southern part of the country maintained a precarious semi-independence under the Theban rulers of the Seventeenth Dynasty. Most of the Hyksos seem to have adhered to Canaanite burial practices and so evidence for coffin development in this period comes mainly from the Theban area. Some of the rectangular coffins are exceptionally long and narrow, with heavily vaulted lids (figure 17). The external decoration, gaudily painted on a black background, includes the eye panel (surrounded by a pectoral-shaped frame) and up to ten columns of text on each of the long sides.

Although rectangular coffins remained popular, many Thebans of this period chose to be buried in a new type of anthropoid case, the so-called *rishi* coffin. These are easily recognisable, both by their ungainly shape and by the characteristic decoration of the lids, which consists chiefly of a huge pair of wings, covering the body from the shoulders to the feet (figure 18). It is this design, representing the deceased shielded by the protective wings of Isis and Nephthys, which has given rise to the modern term '*rishi* coffin', derived from the Arabic word for 'feather'. Additional protection was provided by the vulture Nekhbet and the cobra Wadjet, who are usually depicted on the breast, while the offering formula was generally inscribed down the centre of the lid between the two wings. On *rishi* coffins the dead person is usually represented wearing the royal *nemes* headdress, irrespective of his rank in life.

Some of these coffins were put together from small pieces of wood but others were hollowed out of tree trunks. The majority were of mediocre workmanship, but those of the kings and queens of the Seventeenth Dynasty, buried at Dra Abu el-Naga, were beautifully finished, with a layer of gold leaf and inlaid eyes (figure 19).

Royal coffins of the Eighteenth Dynasty

Following in the traditions of the Seventeenth Dynasty, New Kingdom royal coffins continued to be made on the *rishi* pattern, though in a modified form. The changes are illustrated by the coffins of King Ahmose and his son Prince Siamun, recovered from the Royal Cache at Deir el-Bahri (figure 20). The wig is of the tripartite 'divine' type and the bodily proportions are much more faithfully reproduced. Instead of being covered by two complete wings, the body now appears entirely sheathed in plumage, back and front, rather as if the deceased were dressed in an enveloping garment of feathers. The shoulders and torso are covered with overlapping rows of small scale-like feathers, while over the legs are rows of long feathers — the two zones representing the upper

20. Coffin of King Ahmose. Deir el-Bahri, early Eighteenth Dynasty. (Cairo CG 61002; from Daressy, *Cercueils des Cachettes Royales*, Cairo, 1909, plate III.)

21. Coffin of Queen Ahmose-Nefertari. Deir el-Bahri, early Eighteenth Dynasty. (Cairo CG 61003; from Daressy, *Cercueils des Cachettes Royales*, Cairo, 1909, plate III.)

and lower sections of a falcon's plumage.

A similar design occurs on the outer coffins of three queens of the family of Ahmose: his mother, Aahotep; his wife, Ahmose-Nefertari; and Meryet-Amun, the consort of Amenophis I. These are of exceptionally large size, being over 3 metres high, and have several features of interest. Those of Aahotep and Nefertari, which are made of cartonnage, represent the queen wearing a long wig surmounted by a tall feathered headdress — the only examples of this feature on a coffin (figure 21). That of Meryet-Amun is of similar design but is made of cedar wood and lacks the twin feathers. An important innovation, seen for the first time on these three coffins, was the representation of the hands crossed on the breast, underlining the deceased's identification with Osiris. All three queens probably had inner coffins of smaller size, but only that of Meryet-Amun has survived. It displays less originality than the outer coffin, being somewhat top-heavy in appearance and lacking the crossed hands.

By the middle of the Eighteenth Dynasty the typical burial ensemble of a pharaoh comprised three coffins, nested one inside the other. Although only Tutankhamun's group has survived intact, the battered second coffin of Tuthmosis III from the Royal Cache must have formed part of a similar set, and the internal dimensions of the stone sarcophagi indicate that other kings were similarly equipped. Whereas the first and second coffins of Tutankhamun are very deep and have a bulky appearance, the innermost coffin, of solid gold, is perfect both in its proportions and in the standard of craftsmanship which it displays (figure 22). All three represent the young king grasping royal sceptres and adorned with the vulture and uraeus on his brow. The first and second coffins are of wood, covered with gold leaf and inlaid with precious stones and coloured glass. Inlays were also used, more sparingly, on the third coffin. For all their opulence and splendour, the basic design of these coffins is essentially the same as that first seen on the coffin of Ahmose, a bipartite feather pattern enshrouding the whole body. Overlaying this are a central inscription and pairs of vultures (representing Nekhbet and Wadjet) who protect the king with their wings. On the lid of the third coffin winged figures of Isis and Nephthys shielding the king's legs are also depicted.

Private coffins of the Eighteenth Dynasty

The majority of non-royal coffins of the Eighteenth Dynasty have been found at Thebes and at the beginning of this period two main types can be distinguished: anthropoid coffins with *rishi* decoration, and rectangular coffins representing the last manifestations of the Middle Kingdom traditions. These cases had flat or vaulted lids and were usually decorated with geometrical patterns, figures of Isis and Nephthys and Anubis jackals, but they are of poor quality, clumsily painted in gaudy colours. Both types remained in use down to the reign of Tuthmosis III, but by that time an alternative had been developed, a new type of anthropoid case, usually made from sycamore planks but occasionally dug out, which soon achieved great popularity.

22. Inner coffin of Tutankhamun. Valley of the Kings, late Eighteenth Dynasty. (Cairo JE 60671; courtesy of the Griffith Institute, Oxford.)

23. Coffin of Ahmose, son of Nakht. Dra Abu el-Naga, early Eighteenth Dynasty. (Courtesy of the Metropolitan Museum of Art, New York, gift of the Earl of Carnarvon, 1914; 14.10.2ab.)

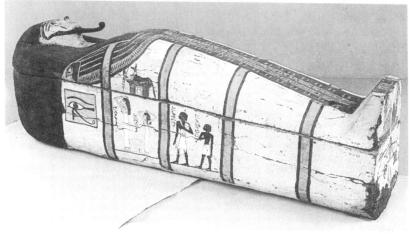

This classic New Kingdom coffin, examples of which are known at least as early as the reign of Tuthmosis I, was the product of a fusion of the main elements of the older mummiform type and the rectangular case. The lid, still copying the traditional appearance of the mummy, was adorned with a tripartite wig and a falcon collar, but it was shallower and less rounded than the lids of Middle Kingdom anthropoid coffins. The case or lower half was generally quite deep, with sides almost vertical, and the base was flattened in the centre since these coffins were buried lying on their backs, not on their sides as in the Middle Kingdom. Part of the ornamentation on the lid and virtually all of that on the case were derived from the decoration of rectangular coffins. The offering formula or a prayer to Nut was inscribed down the centre. Four vertical bands of inscription appeared on the sides and these were positioned so as to join up with the transverse bands on the lid (figure 23). The artist thus killed two birds with one stone, by combining the symbolic 'mummy bandages' of the older anthropoid coffins with the columns containing religious texts, which had been an important feature of rectangular coffins since the First Intermediate Period. These bands now carried the speeches of the main deities, which usually began on the lid and continued without a break down to the bottom of the case. The intervening spaces on the sides were occupied by funeral and offering scenes and, from about the time of Tuthmosis I, by the gods whose speeches appear in the text bands: the sons of Horus, two forms of Anubis and sometimes Thoth. Their positioning follows the arrangement described in chapter 1. Isis and Nephthys were still painted at the foot and the head.

The lateral compartments of the lid were usually left blank but on some coffins they contain Anubis jackals or figures of mourners. The earlier Eighteenth Dynasty coffins have a vulture with outspread wings (Nekhbet?) depicted on the breast below the collar, but from about the reign of Amenophis III the goddess Nut is shown here instead, usually kneeling, and provided with wings which are spread out across the lid. This image is probably a combination of the vulture and goddess motifs and, coinciding with the change, the wording of the prayer to Nut is slightly altered to read: 'Descend, O mother Nut, spread your wings over me . . .'

A general indication of the date of a New Kingdom anthropoid coffin is provided by the colouring. Those of the early Eighteenth Dynasty, down to the reign of Tuthmosis III, have a white-painted ground with unvarnished polychrome decoration. These were succeeded by coffins with a black ground and texts and decoration

24 and 25. Coffin of an unnamed man. Qurna, later Eighteenth Dynasty. (Courtesy of the Trustees of the British Museum; 29580.)

chiefly in gold leaf or yellow paint (figures 24 and 25). This type occurred as early as the reign of Hatshepsut (as exemplified by the coffin of Hatnefer, Cairo J. 66197) and continued into the early Nineteenth Dynasty. Those belonging to very high-ranking persons, such as Yuya and Thuya, parents-in-law of Amenophis III, were gilded all over. At about the end of the Eighteenth Dynasty or at the beginning of the Nineteenth a third type appeared, characterised by polychrome decoration on a yellow ground (chapter 5).

Among other stylistic developments in this period we may note the tendency for the coffin to copy the mummy's shape with increasing accuracy. The black coffins illustrate this clearly, as they generally have better proportions than the earlier white-painted type, some examples of which are very clumsy in form. The depiction of the crossed hands on the lid is first attested on private coffins about the time of Hatshepsut (Cairo J. 66197), but they occur only sporadically before the Nineteenth Dynasty.

During the Eighteenth Dynasty most people seem to have been provided with a single coffin and a mummy mask, but this rule was not invariable. The burials of Maiherperi and Yuya and Thuya in the Valley of the Kings revealed that for high-ranking individuals sets of up to four coffins were available. The outermost was shaped like a shrine (an appropriate resting place for one who was identified with Osiris) and mounted on wooden sledge runners, like the catafalques which were used to transport the mummy to the tomb. Whether the specimens belonging to Yuya and Thuya were used for this purpose is open to question, since there is evidence to suggest that they were assembled in the tomb.

5
The Ramesside Period

Relatively few coffins can be assigned to the Nineteenth and Twentieth Dynasties. Many of the tombs of the high officials probably still await discovery in the Memphite necropolis, so we are mainly dependent on material from Thebes. Unfortunately, the Ramesside tombs there have suffered so badly at the hands of plunderers that very few well preserved coffins have survived. The most notable exceptions, however, are those of Sennedjem and his family, discovered in 1886 in an intact sepulchre at Deir el-Medina and now divided between Cairo, New York and Berlin.

Anthropoid coffins were now the norm, although sometimes a wooden shrine-shaped catafalque was also provided (that of Khonsu, son of Sennedjem, being perhaps the finest surviving example). The old black-painted coffins continued in use into the reign of Ramesses II, but they were gradually superseded by the new type, introduced around the end of the Eighteenth Dynasty. These were painted in bright colours, mainly red and blue, on a yellow ground and covered with a clear varnish, which, having darkened through time, gives the decoration a predominantly yellowish tone. The lids were decorated with a winged Nut, while the spaces between the text bands began to be occupied by scenes of the deceased offering to gods, episodes from the funeral ceremonies and other depictions reminiscent of tomb paintings (figure 26). The exterior of the case was generally decorated with figures of Thoth and the sons of Horus, as in the Eighteenth Dynasty. Some changes in points of detail are worthy of note. The crossed hands became a standard feature and the clenched fists often hold religious emblems; the floral collar usually covers the forearms, and yet the hands protrude through it in a rather implausible way. The headdresses represent a break with formal tradition, for instead of the tripartite wig associated with the gods and with the dead most of the better Ramesside coffins have the kinds of headdress that the fashion-conscious nobleman and his wife were wearing at the time. The women favoured a heavy wig with straight masses of hair brought forward over both shoulders and held together with horizontal bands, while the type worn by men consisted of two lateral 'flaps' of hair swept backwards to the shoulders and then folded forward over the breast.

Mummy-boards

In this period one or two coffins per person seems to have been

Egyptian Coffins

26. Outer and inner coffins of Henutmehit. Thebes, Nineteenth Dynasty. (Courtesy of the Trustees of the British Museum; 48001.)

usual and a new element was added to the burial equipment: a full-length mummy-shaped covering which was placed directly over the bandaged corpse. Two different types of these 'mummy-boards' were in use during the Ramesside Period. The earlier version consisted of two separate pieces made of wood or cartonnage. The upper half comprised the face mask, collar and crossed arms, while the lower portion was decorated like a coffin lid, with winged Nut and bands of inscription dividing the field into compartments containing scenes of the deceased before various gods (figure 27). The background to the scenes was cut away, allowing the colour of the mummy's shroud to show through. These openwork mummy-boards seem to date mainly from the reign of Ramesses II. Several

27. Inner coffin and open-work mummy-board of Henutmehit. Thebes, Nineteenth Dynasty. (Courtesy of the Trustees of the British Museum; 48001.)

28. Mummy-board of Khay showing the owner as a living person. Deir el-Medina, Nineteenth or Twentieth Dynasty. (Brussels E.6878; courtesy of the Musées Royaux d'Art et d'Histoire, Brussels, and A C L, Brussels.)

29. Coffin of Tairsekheru, a child. Nineteenth or Twentieth Dynasty. (Courtesy of the Royal Museum of Scotland, Edinburgh; 1887. 597.)

30. Coffin of Nesamun. Thebes, reign of Ramesses XI, *c.*1098-1070 BC. (Courtesy of Leeds City Museum; D 426. 1960.)

examples have been discovered at Deir el-Medina and in 1985 a damaged specimen was found in the tomb of Iurudef at Saqqara.

The second type of mummy-board consisted of a single rigid cover of stuccoed and painted wood, reaching from head to foot. The tendency towards a more realistic depiction of the deceased, noted above in connection with the wigs of Ramesside coffins, was now developed much further, for these boards represented the owner not as a mummy but as a living person, dressed in the clothes of daily life (figure 28). The men wear a white linen kilt and sometimes a long robe as well; they have the short square beard and the hands may be laid on the thighs or crossed on the breast. Women wear an elaborately pleated dress and may have rich jewellery; one hand is held by the side and the other flexed across the breast. Occasionally this kind of decoration appears on the lid of the coffin itself and among the examples are some interesting miniature versions made for children (figure 29). This paradoxical fashion for representing the dead as living people also influenced the design of shabtis, and a few sarcophagi of high officials from this period show the same tendency.

The Twentieth Dynasty

The next major change in coffin design seems to have occurred around the end of the Twentieth Dynasty. A number of very fine Theban specimens from this period have survived (figure 30) and these reveal significant developments. The 'daily dress' design goes out of fashion and the emphasis reverts to the depiction of the deceased as an idealised divine being, mummified, with the tripartite wig, the curled 'Osirian' beard and the arms crossed on the breast. The bands of inscription on the lid increase in number and no longer occupy the traditional positions of the main 'mummy bandages'. They now serve simply as borders for the vignettes and it is notable that they do not continue on to the case — the link between the two halves of the coffin was thus broken. The case exterior carries a horizontal strip of vignettes with a frieze or inscription above and below. The traditional motifs (such as the sons of Horus) continued to appear but in the following period they were gradually reduced in prominence and either restricted to one end of each side or omitted completely, as new scenes began to be added. The mummy-board, while remaining a standard part of the ensemble, now became virtually a copy of the coffin lid, with bands of inscription and brightly coloured figured scenes.

40

31. Coffin of the *wab* priest Amenhotep. Probably from Thebes, Twenty-first Dynasty. (Courtesy of the Rijksmuseum van Oudheden, Leiden; M.5, Inv. AMM 16.)

32. Horus presents the *udjat* eye to the enthroned Osiris. Coffin of Tayuhenut, probably from Thebes, Twenty-first Dynasty. (Bolton Museum 69.30.)

6
The Twenty-first Dynasty

The royal burials of Tanis

At the death of Ramesses XI (c. 1070 BC) the throne passed to the Twenty-first Dynasty, a line of pharaohs who ruled from the Delta city of Tanis. The extensive plundering of the New Kingdom royal tombs in the Valley of the Kings had by now become a national scandal and so, in an attempt to safeguard their own bodies and funerary furniture from robbers, the kings of the Twenty-first and Twenty-second Dynasties were interred within the temple precinct at their capital. The excavation of their tombs by Pierre Montet in 1939-40 revealed a number of undisturbed and partially plundered burials, the richest finds being made in the tomb of Psusennes I (c. 1039-991 BC). This king had been buried in two stone sarcophagi, originally made in the New Kingdom, which contained a mummiform coffin of solid silver overlaid with gold, resembling in its general appearance the inner coffin of Tutankhamun. It was made in two halves, which were secured by tenons and rivets, and represents Psusennes as Osiris, wearing the *nemes* headdress and divine beard and grasping the royal sceptres in his crossed hands.

In its external decoration this coffin displays a striking conservatism. The basic design of the lid is a bipartite feather pattern, almost identical to that of the second and third coffins of Tutankhamun, which were made over three centuries earlier. The vulture of Nekhbet (?) is also present, stretched out over the king's breast, though her companion, Wadjet, is here replaced by two falcons which spread their wings over the lower breast. Within the coffin were a finely crafted gold mask and a large sheet of gold placed over the body, resembling the mummy-boards used in private burials. Upon it were represented the king's hands grasping sceptres, a large ram-headed falcon and bands of inscription crossing at right angles.

The richness of Psusennes' burial equipment demonstrates that the royal family at this period was by no means impoverished, although the days of Egypt's prestige as a leading international power were long past. Indeed, the burial of Wen-djeba-en-djed, a contemporary of Psusennes I who was interred in the king's tomb, was also extremely opulent, with a gilded wooden outer coffin and an inner one of solid silver. These were badly decomposed but enough fragments survived to show that their decoration closely resembled that of the contemporary Theban coffins.

Theban coffins

The study of Theban coffins of this period is greatly facilitated by the discovery at Deir el-Bahri of hundreds of specimens belonging to the priests of Amun. These can be dated more precisely than the coffins of earlier periods, since in many instances the mummy's bandages and trappings bore inscriptions which provide a reliable indication of the date of the burial.

The normal provision for a private individual at this period was two anthropoid wooden coffins and a mummy-board, though for persons of modest means the outer coffin was sometimes dispensed with. In shape, decoration and exterior colouring they resemble those of the late Ramesside Period. The scenes were painted in bright colours on a yellow ground and the varnish, which was washed on even more generously than before, imparted an orange-yellow tone to the whole surface. Some of the figures on the lid were moulded in plaster and painted, to give the impression of raised relief and possibly to imitate inlays. The coffins of men and women were very similar, the only distinguishing features being the wig, face and hands (clenched for men, open for women). Below the arms Nut is usually shown spreading her wings over the body, and the lower part of the lid is divided into compartments filled with a bewildering variety of gods, religious emblems and short texts, crammed into every available space (figure 31). This overcrowding of the coffin surfaces with funerary symbolism is typical of the period.

After the New Kingdom decorated tomb chapels virtually ceased to be produced and so the most essential scenes and texts were transferred to coffins, funerary papyri and wooden stelae. A reorganisation of funerary iconography seems to have occurred at about the end of the Twentieth Dynasty, resulting in a new repertoire of scenes. The main theme of most of them was that of rebirth and they are drawn chiefly from Osirian and solar mythology. Many of them were already familiar from the Book of the Dead and other compositions and had been popular elements in New Kingdom tomb decoration: the journey of the deceased into the netherworld, with the judgement before Osiris and demon gatekeepers. Also popular were images of the sunrise, the journey of the solar barque and extracts from the Litany of Re. There were, besides, quite new motifs such as the separation of Geb (earth) and Nut (sky), and Osiris enthroned above a double staircase (figure 32), in which the mummy of the deceased is sometimes shown. Both scenes symbolise resurrection. In addition there were older established subjects such as the sons of Horus, the deceased offer-

33. At left the deceased offers to Khefthernebes and the Hathor cow; at right the four sons of Horus in a shrine. Coffin of Tayuhenut, probably from Thebes, Twenty-first Dynasty. (Bolton Museum 69.30.)

ing to Osiris and other gods, the Hathor cow in the necropolis (figure 33) and a tree goddess providing the deceased with life-giving water. Most of the coffins of this period have a selection from this wide range of subjects, usually in a horizontal strip around the case.

From the end of the Twentieth Dynasty the interior of the coffin was regularly decorated, usually with brightly coloured scenes on a dark red ground. On the floor we often find a profile figure of the Goddess of the West (a form of Hathor) or the Djed pillar, a very ancient device which by the New Kingdom had come to be associated with Osiris. Believed to represent the god's backbone, it symbolised stability and endurance and was regarded as a particularly appropriate adornment for the floor of the coffin, against which the mummy's spine rested (figure 34). These designs were surrounded by small images of gods, which also covered the internal walls. On many coffins of the later Twenty-first Dynasty the deceased's *Ba* is shown above the mummy's head in its usual form of a human-headed bird.

Changes in some of the main features provide clues to the dating of coffins within this period. From about 1000 BC the collar becomes larger and covers the arms, so that only the hands are exposed, and in the area below this two or three winged deities are depicted where Nut alone appeared before. Towards the end of the Twenty-first Dynasty the red leather 'mummy braces' which were

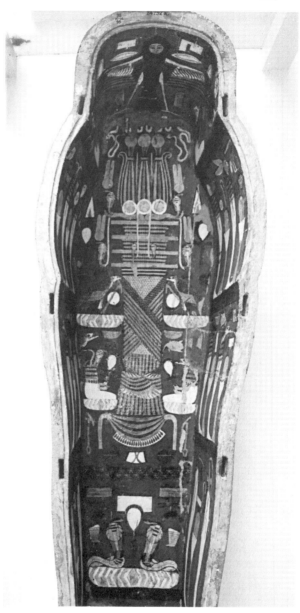

34. *Ba* bird and Djed pillar painted inside the coffin of Bakenmut. Deir el-Bahri, Twenty-first Dynasty. (Courtesy of the Trustees of the British Museum; 24792.)

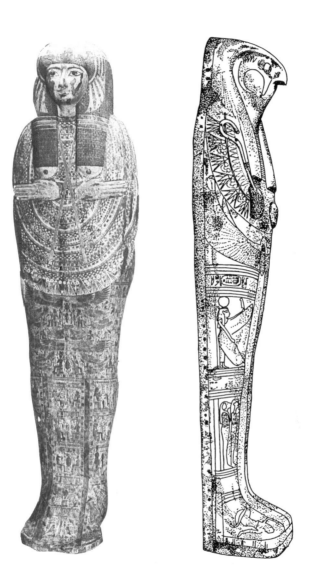

35. Lid of the coffin of Iamut with large collar and painted 'mummy braces'. Late Twenty-first or early Twenty-second Dynasty. (City of Bristol Museum and Art Gallery; H.4633.)

36. Lid of the silver coffin of King Heqakheperre Shoshenq II. Tanis, early Twenty-second Dynasty, *c*.890 BC. (Cairo JE 72154; after Montet, *Les Constructions et le Tombeau de Psousennes*, Paris, 1951, plate XVIII.)

part of burial equipment at this time begin to be painted on the coffin collar and there is a tendency for the scenes to become still more overcrowded (figure 35).

In the later years of the tenth century BC (early Twenty-second Dynasty) many coffins of poor workmanship were produced and the rich variety of mythological representations was giving way to the monotonous repetition of nondescript offering scenes. However, shortly before the disappearance of the 'yellow' coffins there was a last burst of inspiration, exemplified by a group of specimens which show deliberate use of certain motifs taken from the tomb decoration of the Ramesside Period, such as the Book of Amduat, relatives offering to the deceased, and the deified Amenophis I. The lids of these coffins are mostly of the type with 'mummy braces' and a very large collar, and the decoration of the floor is often arranged in a series of registers. Remarkably, the internal paintings are often very beautifully done, whereas those on the exterior are mediocre or poor.

Very few private coffins of this period have been discovered elsewhere in Upper Egypt but a few specimens are known from Akhmim and Kom Ombo and another was discovered at Amarna in 1984. In their construction and decoration they are very similar to the contemporary Theban examples, which suggests that the same basic traditions were influential throughout most of the Nile valley at this time.

7
The Libyan Period

Royal coffins of the Twenty-second Dynasty

Under the Libyan pharaohs of the Twenty-second Dynasty major changes occurred in the design of both royal and private coffins. The burial of King Heqakheperre Shoshenq II (died *c.*890 BC), found in the antechamber of Psusennes I's tomb at Tanis, illustrates the nature of some of the innovations. Shoshenq's silver coffin is mummiform and the crossed hands hold royal sceptres, but in place of the traditional idealised face wearing the *nemes* we now find the head of a falcon and the striated tripartite wig of a god (figure 36), perhaps alluding to the king's role as the incarnation of Horus. The traditional feathered decoration of the body was also abandoned; instead, a ram-headed falcon spreads its wings over the breast, while below this bands of inscription divide the field into large rectangular compartments containing figures of gods and goddesses. When the coffin was opened the royal mummy was found enclosed in a poorly preserved casing of gilded cartonnage, possibly modelled over a wooden frame. In its original state this had been very similar to the silver coffin, both in its decoration and in its having a falcon's head. This latter peculiarity seems to have been typical of the coffins of Twenty-second Dynasty pharaohs: Montet recovered fragments of a similar cartonnage from the plundered sarcophagus of Osorkon II, and the Theban high priest of Amun Harsiese, who claimed royal titles, was buried at Medinet Habu *c.*860 BC in a sarcophagus with a falcon-headed lid.

Thebes and Middle Egypt

In the southern part of Egypt, too, a major change occurred in the second half of the tenth century BC, affecting all aspects of funerary equipment and all levels of society. It is at Thebes that this change can be observed most clearly. At the beginning of the Twenty-second Dynasty the long-established 'yellow' coffins were still being produced, but by the reign of Osorkon I (*c.*924-889 BC) these had been superseded by new types which were quite different in form, construction and style of decoration. The shape of the wooden coffins was simplified; after a few years the crossed hands ceased to be represented on the lid and the modelling of the elbows was eliminated. Instead of the old ensemble of one or two coffins and a mummy-board, Theban priests and officials were now provided with one, two or three wooden coffins and a one-piece cartonnage mummy case as an innermost envelope for the body.

These cartonnage cases, which are typical of the Libyan Period, are interesting both for the ingenious method of their manufacture and for the very attractive painted scenes with which they are decorated (figure 37). Although some cartonnages fit very closely around the mummy, in others the body is found to be considerably shorter than the case. Apparently then, the cartonnage was not moulded around the body itself, but rather over a disposable core of mud and straw which reproduced the approximate shape and dimensions of the average mummy. This core was coated with coarse plaster and several layers of linen soaked in gum were applied, covering it completely except for the section at the base of the feet. A narrow vertical opening was also left at the rear and, once the final layer of linen had been applied, this rear slit was carefully opened out and the core removed in pieces, leaving a hollow mummiform shell of plaster and gummed linen. The exterior was then coated with gesso and holes were punched in the edges of the rear flaps. The mummy was apparently inserted before the case was decorated, the rear flaps being drawn together by two strings laced through the holes from head to foot. A wooden board was pegged on beneath the feet and thus the mummy was sealed inside. The case was then ready to be decorated.

The cartonnage mummy case had a number of advantages. It was probably relatively cheap and easy to produce, while the medium of gummed linen and plaster was easy to model and a lifelike, if idealised, face mask, complete with wig, could be moulded before the material hardened. However, these cases were not substitutes for genuine coffins, since they were always placed inside wooden cases, which were frequently made of costly imported timber. One-piece cartonnages are first attested at Thebes in the reign of Osorkon I and already by this time they display a technical and stylistic maturity which in no way suggests that they were a recent invention (figure 38). Since they were already in use at Tanis by the early Twenty-second Dynasty it is possible that the type originated in the north of Egypt and was introduced into the south only when it was fully developed.

This change in burial practices coincided with another reorganisation of the funerary iconography, which is suggestive of a change of emphasis in attitudes towards the afterlife. On coffins, much of the new decoration consisted, as before, of symbols of rebirth and divine protection, but there was a preference for motifs with a general beneficial meaning rather than specific extracts from the old-established funerary literature. Hence there is a profusion of winged deities and divine fetishes, usually arranged in symmetrical

37. Coffin and cartonnage case of the lady Tjentdinebu. Probably from Thebes, early Twenty-second Dynasty. (Courtesy of the National Museum of Ireland, Dublin; 1881.2228.)

38. Cartonnage case of Tjentmutengebtiu with decoration in horizontal registers. Thebes, early Twenty-second Dynasty. (Courtesy of the Trustees of the British Museum; 22939.)

groupings, while most of the typical scenes found on coffins of the eleventh and tenth centuries BC were swept away. Only a few of the more popular images, such as the Hathor cow and the presentation of the deceased to Osiris or Re, were retained, but even these appeared in new locations. There was also a noticeable increase in the prominence of solar symbolism. Re-Harakhty appears in vignettes more often than Osiris, winged sun-disks and falcons representing the solar Horus are common and a scarab is usually painted on the top of the head. Deities associated with the Memphite area also gain new prominence on Theban coffins, as exemplified by the frequent depiction of the barque of the god Sokar and the painting

39. Coffin of the singer Panesy. The scenes and texts are painted in yellow on a black ground. Probably from Thebes, early-middle Twenty-second Dynasty. (Courtesy of the Rijksmuseum van Oudheden, Leiden; M.35.)

40. Outer coffin of the lady Tadi-es. The simple decoration with central inscription is typical of the Libyan Period. Probably from Thebes, Twenty-second Dynasty. (Courtesy of the Rijksmuseum van Oudheden, Leiden, M.61, Inv. AMM 22.)

of the Apis bull beneath the feet. There are many figures of deities but, in contrast to the custom of the Twenty-first Dynasty, the deceased is not often shown before them. Substantial funerary texts almost disappear, inscriptions consisting of little more than offering formulae and labels for the figures.

However, if the content of the decoration was less rich than before, the draughtsmen and painters were allowed much greater freedom in inventing designs and layouts. On some coffin lids the scenes were still arranged in registers or compartments (figure 39), but large, boldly painted deities and symbols were also frequent. A design particularly popular on cartonnages consisted chiefly of two large falcons (one with the head of a ram) stretching their wings obliquely up to the shoulders and down towards the thighs in an eloquent gesture of protection. There is a new sense of space in the composition of the scenes and the overcrowded appearance of the 'yellow' coffins is avoided. Some coffins, indeed, were very sparsely decorated, with only a single line of inscription on the lid and another around the case (figure 40). The prayer to Nut disappeared and the figure of the goddess was rarely depicted on the outside of the lid. Instead she was drawn on the floor, full-face, with her arms outspread (figure 41). This iconography is unprecedented but is doubtless an expression of the very old concept by which Nut was identified with the whole coffin, enveloping the mummy in a protective embrace. Also characteristic of this period is the representation of a winged headdress over the wig on the coffins and cartonnages of women, a custom which began in the late Twenty-first Dynasty.

There was also a wide variety of colour schemes. Some wooden coffins, like most of the cartonnages, had polychrome decoration on a white ground. Usually only the figures and texts were varnished, the ground being left untouched. This was perhaps done to avoid the overall yellowish discolouration which resulted from the application of a uniform coat of varnish (chapter 6). Other coffins had a much more austere appearance, the ground painted black and the scenes and inscriptions done in yellow or white outline. The layer of plaster on which the decoration was normally painted was sometimes omitted or restricted to the head and collar. On these coffins the figures and inscriptions were painted directly on to the smoothed surface of the wood.

The cemeteries of Middle Egypt have produced relatively few coffins which can be compared with those from Thebes, but a number of burials excavated at Lahun, Sedment and El Hiba yielded material which probably belongs to this period. The mummies were placed in simple wooden coffins with flat lids and sides which usually taper sharply from the shoulders to the feet. The faces, which are often disproportionately small, are surrounded by large wigs which usually have a winged scarab painted on the forehead. These coffins often have hands, frequently decorated with a papyrus motif or a curious chequered design. Otherwise the decoration consists only of a central inscription which is in many cases nonsensical. The coffins contained cartonnage cases similar in form to those from Thebes, but usually with wooden faces and relatively simple designs on a white ground.

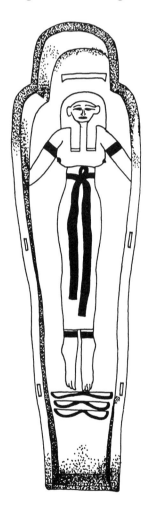

41. The goddess Nut painted full-face on the floor of a Twenty-second Dynasty coffin from Akhmim. (After Koefoed-Petersen, *Catalogue des Sarcophages et Cercueils Égyptiens,* Copenhagen, 1951, plate CII.)

8
The Twenty-fifth Dynasty to the Ptolemaic Period

The Twenty-fifth Dynasty: a transitional phase

Between c.750 BC and c.670 BC (a period corresponding roughly to the Twenty-fifth Dynasty) the style of many items of funerary furniture underwent a gradual transition. The designs and techniques popular in the Libyan Period were transformed or replaced by new ones. There were major changes in the composition of burial ensembles and in the style and subject matter of the decoration. Cartonnage mummy cases became less common and by the beginning of the seventh century BC they had been largely replaced by a new type of inner coffin. This was made of wood, in two halves, and represented the mummy standing on a rectangular pedestal, its back supported by a pillar. In creating this form the craftsman was clearly taking inspiration from statuary and a few decades after the appearance of this type of coffin shabtis underwent a similar transformation, resulting in the creation of a new standard type with back pillar and pedestal. These coffins were always buried in a horizontal position, but it is possible that the pedestal did have a practical function, in helping to keep the coffin steady when it was placed upright at the funeral ceremonies.

Although the pedestal-coffin became the standard type of inner mummy case, it was always enclosed in one or two larger anthropoid cases of more traditional shape, with a flat base and no pedestal. For those who could afford it a new type of outer coffin was also introduced, rectangular in shape, with a vaulted lid and a post at each corner which projected above the rim to the height of the top of the lid (figure 42). It was obviously modelled on a shrine or chapel and as such it has clear affinities with the 'house' coffins of the Old Kingdom and the 'catafalques' of the Eighteenth and Nineteenth Dynasties.

Because this period was one of stylistic transition many of the coffins made at the time display an interesting mixture of old and new features. Not only do we see pedestal-type inner coffins decorated in the manner of cartonnages, with two large falcons on the breast, winged deities and a scarab on the head (figure 43), but also cartonnages and traditional outer coffins with the new style of decoration: larger areas of inscription, more sombre colour schemes and more regular design layouts, with an increasing tendency to present the decoration in neat registers and compartments.

An important factor in the art of this period was 'archaism' — a deliberate revival of techniques, designs and motifs of the Old, Middle and New Kingdoms, which were copied and then interwoven with innovations. This archaising tendency is typical of the Twenty-fifth and Twenty-sixth Dynasties and its effect on the design of coffins is seen in the revival of features like the eye panel on some of the rectangular outer cases and the figures of the sons of Horus, Anubis and Thoth which appear on the sides of anthropoid coffins. More significantly, a great deal of the religious imagery which had disappeared from coffins at the beginning of the Twenty-second Dynasty was now rehabilitated; the winged Nut appears again on the breast of the inner coffin and she is now often shown without wings on the interior of the lid as well. Substantial extracts from the Book of the Dead become common and several of its important vignettes also appear.

As in previous periods, most of the evidence for coffin development at this time comes from Thebes, but there are clear signs that

42. Rectangular outer coffin of Djedthutefankh. Deir el-Bahri, Twenty-fifth Dynasty. (Courtesy of the Visitors of the Ashmolean Museum, Oxford; 1895.153.)

43. Inner coffin of Takhebkhenem, an early example of the type with pedestal and back pillar. The decoration retains designs typical of the Libyan Period. Thebes, Twenty-fifth Dynasty. (Courtesy of the Trustees of the British Museum; 6691.)

the changes which occurred there were part of a general trend
affecting the whole country. The 'four-poster' rectangular coffin
was introduced in Middle Egypt and the Memphite area, as was the
pedestal type of inner case. Sometimes the rectangular coffin was
constructed like a canopy, so that the vaulted top was not detach-
able, and it was merely placed over the inner coffin, which lay on
a flat base, on the ground or — in one case — on a lion bier. Several
of these 'false sarcophagi' were found by Petrie at Lahun. The
anthropoid inner coffins here had white bodies decorated with rib-
bing to imitate pleated drapery and several plain white pedestal-
coffins of about this period, from Lahun and El Hiba, were probably derived from this type.

The Twenty-sixth Dynasty
By the beginning of the Twenty-sixth Dynasty (664 BC) the new
repertoire of coffin types was fully established. The coffins were
generally provided in sets of two or three, comprising an inner case
with pedestal, an anthropoid intermediary coffin and an outer
case, either anthropoid again or of the 'four-poster' type. The
intermediary coffins resembled the sparsely decorated examples of
the Libyan Period, with coloured head and collar and brief inscriptions painted directly on to the wood. The outer and inner mummiform coffins were covered with linen, plastered and painted in
bright colours on a white or yellow ground. The decoration of the
outer coffin lids consisted mainly of registers filled with scenes such
as the judgement and the mummy lying on a bier, alternating with
bands of short text columns. A large inscription was usual around
the case, while the interior was frequently decorated with a figure
of the god Ptah-Sokar-Osiris (figure 44).
The rectangular type of outer coffin was usually decorated with
texts and figures of deities in shrines, while the lid often had two
depictions of the solar barque being towed by gods. The inner coffins received the greatest concentration of decoration. Two main
types of lid design can be distinguished. The first has a figure of Nut
below the collar, often above a narrow band showing the judgement of the deceased. Below this the surface is divided into three
sections, the central one containing vertical columns of text and a
small vignette from the Book of the Dead, while the two lateral
areas contain figures of deities accompanied by their recitations
(figure 45). The best known examples with this design have been
found at Deir el-Bahri and belonged to the priests of Amun and
Monthu and their families. On the second type of lid layout (found
mainly on the coffins of persons of lower rank) the winged Nut and

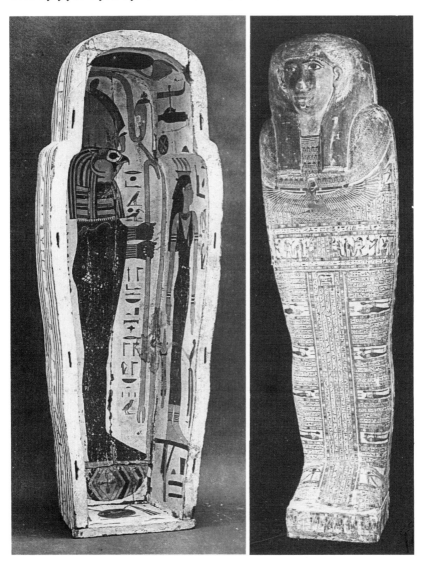

44. Anthropoid outer coffin of Neskhonsupakhered with a figure of the god Ptah-Sokar-Osiris on the floor. Thebes, Twenty-fifth or early Twenty-sixth Dynasty. (Courtesy of the Trustees of the British Museum; 47975.)

45. Inner coffin of the lady Tefiut. Probably from Thebes, Twenty-sixth Dynasty. (Courtesy of the National Museum of Ireland, Dublin; 1888.23.)

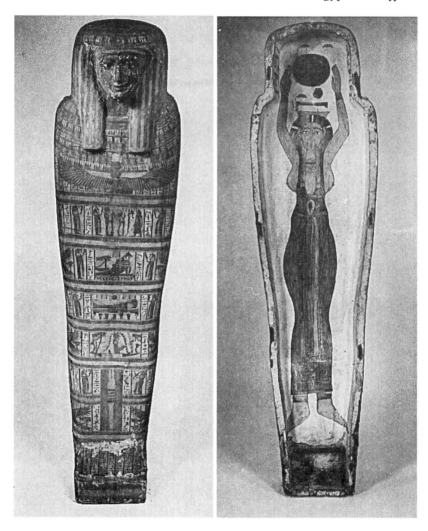

46 and 47. Lid of the inner coffin of Inamun-nefnebu; on the interior the goddess Nut stretched above the deceased. Probably from Thebes, late Twenty-fifth or early Twenty-sixth Dynasty. (Courtesy of the Rijksmuseum van Oudheden, Leiden; M.30, Inv. AMM 1.)

48. Back of the inner coffin of Kakaiu. Probably from Thebes, late Twenty-fifth or early Twenty-sixth Dynasty. (Courtesy of the Rijksmuseum van Oudheden, Leiden; M.65, Inv. AMM 4.)

judgement scene are followed by further depictions in horizontal bands. In the area below the knees are figures of gods arranged symmetrically on either side of the Abydos fetish — an emblem associated with Osiris (figure 46). The inscriptions tend to be brief, and lengthy extracts from the Book of the Dead are rare.

The rear of the inner coffin, whatever the nature of the lid design, was usually decorated either with a large Djed pillar or with a series of text columns (figure 48). The interior was often covered with extracts from the Book of the Dead or figures of Nut (figure 47) and Hathor. Nephthys often appears at the top of the head, as in earlier periods. She is sometimes counterbalanced by Isis at the

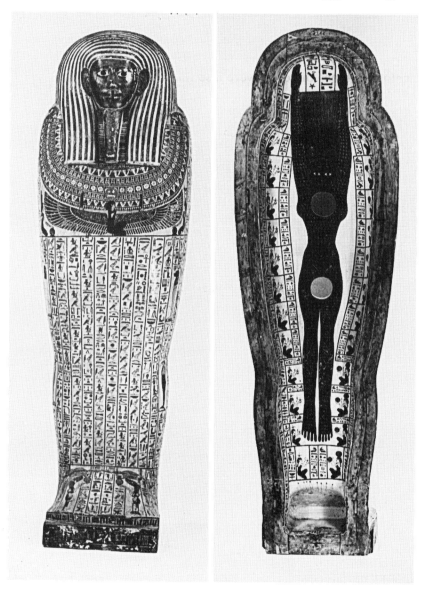

49 and 50. Lid of the coffin of Peftjau-Neith; on the interior Nut with star-studded body (cf figure 47). The small female figures personify the hours of day and night. Probably from Saqqara, Twenty-sixth Dynasty. (Courtesy of the Rijksmuseum van Oudheden, Leiden; M.13, Inv. AMM 5.)

base of the foot, but this area may instead carry the scene of the Apis bull bearing the mummy of the deceased on its back — a survival from the Libyan Period.

These styles continued at Thebes into the sixth century and analogous types of coffin were also made at other sites in Upper Egypt, notably Akhmim, and in the Memphite region. A fine specimen, probably from Saqqara, is that of Peftjau-Neith (figures 49 and 50). The long inscription on the lid is the dominant feature here, the hieroglyphs being drawn with great care and painted in brilliant colours. As occasionally happened in the Twenty-sixth Dynasty, the face is painted green to stress the deceased's identification with Osiris. Nut spreads her wings over the breast, and she also appears inside the lid, this time as a naked woman, her arms stretched above her head, with a dark-coloured star-studded body — a clear allusion to her role as the protective sky goddess.

The Persian Period to the Ptolemaic Period

Very few datable burials have been found from the period between the Persian conquest of Egypt in 525 BC and the middle of the fourth century BC but a relatively large number of coffins can be assigned to the Thirtieth Dynasty and early Ptolemaic Period (fourth to early third centuries BC). The anthropoid cases of this period have several distinctive characteristics. The head and body tend to be disproportionately large and the collar, which covers the upper part of the torso, begins below the ends of the wig. It has large falcon-head terminals and a pectoral is often depicted in the centre. The decoration of the coffins varies little, the main subjects being the winged Nut, the mummy on a lion-headed bier, jackals seated on shrines, and rows of netherworld genii holding knives. The inscriptions, too, are standardised and frequently include short extracts from the Pyramid Texts in addition to portions of the Book of the Dead. The coffins are often brightly coloured and gilding was applied to the faces, even of quite mediocre specimens.

The mummies of this period often had masks and decorated plaques of cartonnage which were placed over the outer wrappings and held in position by elaborate bandaging. These coverings normally comprised a falcon-collar (sometimes with a figure of Nut attached), an 'apron' over the legs and a footcase. Several good-quality burials belonging to this period have been found at Thebes and Akhmim, consisting of two anthropoid coffins and cartonnage mummy coverings. The outer coffins are clumsy in appearance, with large heads sunk into the shoulders, voluminous wigs and large collars (figure 51). The pedestal (which now appears on both

51. Outer coffin of Nesmin. Akhmim, Thirtieth Dynasty or Early Ptolemaic Period. (Courtesy of the Trustees of the British Museum; 29582.)

52. Inner coffin of Nesmin. Akhmim, Thirtieth Dynasty or Early Ptolemaic Period. (Courtesy of the Trustees of the British Museum; 29581.)

outer and inner coffins) is large and deep. The decoration, selected from the subjects mentioned above, may be polychrome or painted mainly in yellow on a black ground. The inner coffin is normally well proportioned and has carved decoration (figure 52). The head and collar are brightly coloured, but otherwise the decoration usually consists only of a central inscription flanked by figures of the sons of Horus — all painted on to the bare wood.

As the Ptolemaic Period wore on, these coffin types went out of use, to be replaced by new forms in which the traditional Egyptian motifs became increasingly mixed with Hellenistic features. Further developments took place under the Romans, but these lie outside the scope of this book.

9
Further reading

Apart from museum catalogues, there is no other book in English which deals exclusively with Egyptian coffins. The following works contain valuable sections on coffin style at different periods.

Andrews, C. *Egyptian Mummies*. British Museum Publications, 1984.

Bonnet, H. *Reallexikon der Ägyptischen Religionsgeschichte*. Berlin, 1952.

Bruyère, B. *Rapport sur les Fouilles de Deir el Médineh (1934-1935)*. Fouilles de l'Institut Francais d'Archéologie Orientale du Caire XV, Cairo, 1937.

Carter, H., and Carnarvon, Earl of. *Five Years' Explorations at Thebes. A Record of Work Done 1907-11*. London, 1912.

Hayes, W. C. *Royal Sarcophagi of the XVIII Dynasty*. Princeton University Press, 1935.

Hayes, W. C. *The Scepter of Egypt*, I-II. Metropolitan Museum of Art, New York, 1953, 1959.

Mace, A. C., and Winlock, H. E. *The Tomb of Senebtisi at Lisht*. Metropolitan Museum of Art, New York, 1916.

Spencer, A. J. *Death in Ancient Egypt*. Penguin, 1982.

The titles listed below are of a more specialised nature:

Faulkner, R. O. *The Ancient Egyptian Coffin Texts*, I-III. Aris and Phillips, 1973, 1977, 1978.

Lapp, G. 'Särge des AR und MR', *Lexikon der Ägyptologie*, volume V (1983), 430-4.

Niwiński, A. 'Sarg NR-SpZt.', *Lexikon der Ägyptologie*, volume V (1983), 434-68.

Roveri, A. M. Donadoni. *I Sarcofagi Egizi dalle Origini alla Fine dell' Antico Regno*. Rome, 1969.

Schmidt, V. *Sarkofager, Mumiekister, og Mumiehylstre i det Gamle Aegypten. Typologisk Atlas*. Copenhagen, 1919.

10
Museums

The following list includes museums with important collections of Egyptian coffins. Intending visitors are advised to find out the times of opening before making a special journey.

United Kingdom

Ashmolean Museum of Art and Archaeology, Beaumont Street, Oxford OX1 2PH. Telephone: 0865 278000.

Bolton Museum and Art Gallery, Le Mans Crescent, Bolton, Lancashire BL1 1SE. Telephone: 0204 22311 extension 2191.

British Museum, Great Russell Street, London WC1B 3DG. Telephone: 01-636 1555.

City of Bristol Museum and Art Gallery, Queen's Road, Bristol, Avon BS8 1RL. Telephone: 0272 299771.

Fitzwilliam Museum, Trumpington Street, Cambridge CB2 1RB. Telephone: 0223 332900.

Leicestershire Museum and Art Gallery, 96 New Walk, Leicester LE1 6TD. Telephone: 0533 554100.

Liverpool Museum, William Brown Street, Liverpool, L3 8EN. Telephone: 051-207 0001 or 5451.

Manchester Museum, The University of Manchester, Oxford Road, Manchester M13 9PL. Telephone: 061-273 3333.

Petrie Museum of Egyptian Archaeology, University College London, Gower Street, London WC1E 6BT. Telephone: 01-387 7050 extension 2884.

Royal Museum of Scotland, Chambers Street, Edinburgh EH1 1JF. Telephone: 031-225 7534.

Belgium

Musées Royaux d'Art et d'Histoire, Avenue J. F. Kennedy, 1040 Brussels.

Egypt

Egyptian Museum, Tahrir Square, Cairo.

France

Musée du Louvre, Palais du Louvre, 75003 Paris.

Germany East

Ägyptisches Museum, Staatliche Museen, Bodestrasse 1-3, 102 Berlin.

Italy
Museo Egizio, Palazzo dell' Accademia delle Scienze, Via Accademia delle Scienze 6, Turin.

Netherlands
Rijksmuseum van Oudheden, Rapenburg 28, 2311 EW, Leiden, Zuid Holland.

United States of America
Metropolitan Museum of Art, 5th Avenue at 82nd Street, New York, NY 10028.
Museum of Fine Arts, Huntington Avenue, Boston, Massachusetts 02115.

Acknowledgements

My researches on Egyptian coffins have been greatly facilitated by the staff of many museums who have allowed me to study specimens in their collections and I wish to express my gratitude to all of them. For permission to reproduce the photographs which appear in this book I am indebted to Bolton Museum and Art Gallery; City of Bristol Museum and Art Gallery; the Fitzwilliam Museum, Cambridge; the Griffith Institute, Oxford; Leeds City Museum; the Metropolitan Museum of Art, New York; Musées Royaux d'Art et d'Histoire, Brussels; the National Museum of Ireland; Rijksmuseum van Oudheden, Leiden; the Trustees of the British Museum; the Trustees of the National Museums of Scotland; and the Visitors of the Ashmolean Museum, Oxford. Special thanks are also due to Mrs Barbara Adams, Miss Janine Bourriau, Mr Vivian Davies, Miss Elizabeth Pirie, Dr Maarten Raven, Dr Nicholas Reeves, Dr Jeffrey Spencer, Mrs Angela Thomas and Miss Helen Whitehouse for their prompt and generous assistance, and to Mr Graham Norrie for expert help with several of the photographic illustrations. The dynastic chronology is based on that of Dr William J. Murnane and acknowledgement is made to him and Penguin Books for its use here.

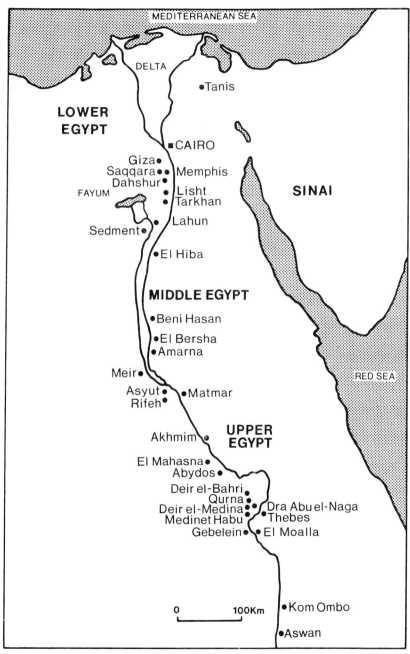

53. Map of Egypt, showing the location of sites mentioned in the text.

Index

Page numbers in italic refer to illustrations